Original title:
Searching for Meaning in a Cup of Coffee

Copyright © 2025 Creative Arts Management OÜ
All rights reserved.

Author: Alec Davenport
ISBN HARDBACK: 978-1-80566-084-2
ISBN PAPERBACK: 978-1-80566-379-9

Cup Half Full

In the morning, I take a sip,
Steam rises up, like dreams on a trip.
The mug whispers tales, oh so bold,
Of caffeine adventures yet to unfold.

A dash of cream, a sprinkle of spice,
Each drop of joy, oh, isn't it nice?
I ponder life's questions, where to start,
While dodging the coffee grounds of the heart.

Brews of Hope and Reflection

I brewed a thought, let it steep,
A splash of laughter, in a world so deep.
The cup grins wide, full of cheer,
With each little sip, problems disappear.

Do I want it black, or sweet like a pie?
My coffee and I, we'll always get by.
Stirring up dreams, with a frothy foamy crown,
In this circus of life, let's never frown.

Bean by Bean, a Journey

The beans collide in a caffeinated dance,
Each sip is a step, another chance.
I travel through flavors, a bold little quest,
On a journey with mugs, in search of the best.

From mocha to latte, a whimsical ride,
With every espresso, my worries subside.
Life's little secrets, brewed hot and fresh,
Like a magic potion, oh, so enmesh.

Guided by the Grind

The grinder hums, a morning tune,
With coffee dreams that make me swoon.
In the swirl of aromas, my thoughts take flight,
A sip of joy, as the sun shines bright.

Each cup tells a story, drizzled in fate,
With each little sip, I procrastinate.
So let's toast to joy in every little pour,
In a world brewed perfect, who could ask for more?

Clarity in Every Pour

A splash of cream, a dash of hope,
Stirring dreams with every slope,
Bitter sips and sweet delight,
Morning magic, feels just right.

Waking up my sleepy mind,
A coffee hug, the best I find,
Dancing thoughts in every swirl,
Each sip's a giggle, a twirl.

Grounds for Reflection

Leftover grounds, a messy fate,
A thinker's muse on my coffee plate,
Steam plumes rise, oh what a show,
Philosophers brewed, let's go, let's go!

Each mug holds a tale to tell,
Of mornings bright, or nights that fell,
Between each sip, I find my jest,
Life's a brew, just like the rest.

Mugs of Memoirs

A chipped old mug, with tales untold,
Housed laughs, and secrets bold,
Sips of wisdom, peeks of past,
In every drop, the shadows cast.

With café lingo, I play detective,
Every slurp, a new perspective,
Bubbles rise like dreams on top,
In this brew, I just can't stop.

Steamy Conversations

Conversations steamier than the brew,
With every cup, I chat with you,
Laughter swirls, as we gulp and grin,
Even the barista joins in on the spin.

Coffee cups, we toast today,
With frothy cheers, we'll sip and stay,
Life's a blend, a playful game,
So pour another, and play the same.

Chasing After the Cream

In my mug, a dance begins,
Chasing cream like it's a sin.
Can I catch that swirl so bright?
Or will it vanish from my sight?

Each drop a dream, so rich and bold,
Tales of warmth, or so I'm told.
With every splash, my heart takes flight,
Sipping magic day and night.

The Sips That Tell a Tale

A steaming cup on chilly days,
Whispers soft in gentle ways.
Each sip unveils a story spun,
Of distant lands and warmth from sun.

Got a secret? Just take a drink!
In the foam, ideas link.
Should I laugh or start to weep?
This coffee's deeper than I keep.

Reflections at the Bottom

At the bottom, what can I find?
A riddle brewed, a truth unlined.
Forgotten dreams or yesterday's laugh?
Still deciding if I should have a half.

A puddle deep, a liquid muse,
In these depths, a lot to lose.
Chocolate swirls or bitter notes,
What do I feel? Is it what I wrote?

Stirred Thoughts and Swayed Ideas

I stir my thoughts into a dance,
With every swirl, I take a chance.
A splash of laughter, a dash of fun,
It's a party brewed for everyone.

With each sip, my mind runs wild,
Are these thoughts from coffee, or my inner child?
Caffeine dreams and sugar highs,
Is it wisdom, or just flat-out lies?

Dissolving into the Darkness

A splash of cream, a dash of glee,
The beans have secrets, come drink with me.
Swirling thoughts, a caffeinated dance,
In this cup, who needs a trance?

Sugar cubes float, like boats at sea,
I ponder life's puzzles, what's wrong with me?
Each sip a riddle, a caffeinated joke,
Is it steeped wisdom or just smoke?

Reflections in a Stained Mug

Oh look, a face in my coffee brew,
Is it my fate or just yesterday's stew?
With every gulp, my worries unwind,
   Is caffeine clarity or just blind?

The tannins laugh, they whisper tight,
Did I brew answers or just lose sight?
In each circle of swirl, truths collide,
  I'm just a mug, let the flavor decide.

The Soulful Sip

A sip so warm, I grunt and sigh,
More beans, less bleak, oh me, oh my!
Is that a thought, or just the brew?
Join me, dear friend, for a chuckle or two.

Steam rising high, a cloud of dreams,
Hiccups of laughter escape in beams.
Caffeinated giggles, oh what a treat,
Life's little questions serve best with heat.

Fleeting Flavor

First taste delightful, a lovely flirt,
Soon it wanes like a far-off smirk.
Every sip leaves me hanging tight,
Chasing joy in a caffeine-fueled night.

Chocolate and hazelnut, bold and bright,
Exploring their depths, oh what a plight!
Do they hold answers, or just bold claims?
Guess I'll just sip, and play silly games.

Lasting Thoughts

I cradle my mug like it's pure gold,
With whirring ideas, both bright and bold.
Each drop, a thought, dipping low and high,
Did I just ponder, or was that a lie?

From bitter to sweet, it's life's little dance,
Maybe this sip is my kind of romance.
Here's to caffeine, the friend that stays,
In funny reflections, we chuckle and play.

Threads of Taste and Time

In the morning sun, I take a sip,
With each warm gulp, my mind does flip.
The coffee's dark, the mug a treasure,
There's joy, it seems, in caffeinated pleasure.

I ponder life through swirling steam,
Can espresso give my dreams a beam?
With froth and foam, my thoughts do twirl,
A latte art, my ideas unfurl.

The creamer dances, oh what a sight,
Like tiny clouds in a sugar fight.
A sprinkle of joy, a dash of cheer,
My cup's philosophy, perfectly clear.

So I sip away, with whimsy and glee,
In every cup, absurdity's key.
For in my brew, I've found a rhyme,
Life's best jokes are brewed in time.

Caffeine Chronicles

In a mug that's warm and round,
I ponder life and its profound.
Is it just beans brewed right?
Or a journey in each light?

A splash of cream, a sprinkle sweet,
Wonders stir, can't feel my feet.
The laughter bubbles, jokes arise,
As I sip my genius prize.

Coffee grounds of dreams awake,
In every gulp, there's more at stake.
Who knew that beans could hold the key?
To mysteries of being free?

With every drop, I seem to find,
Snippets of joy that's redefined.
A sip of giggles, a chuckle loud,
Oh, how I love this steamy crowd!

Musing Over Mocha

Sitting here with a frothy cup,
I wonder if I should just give up.
Is it the chocolate or the grind?
That brings the clarity I hoped to find?

The café chatter, oh what a view,
While I swirl my brew, I ponder too.
Do beans have tales, secrets untold?
With each sip, it starts to unfold.

A swirl of cream, a dash, a laugh,
Are these mere joys or a heartfelt gaff?
The world's a stage; it's all bizarre,
And my drink's the leading star!

With every sip, my thoughts take flight,
Conversations with this liquid light.
Oh, the wisdom that drips from my mug,
Am I brilliant or just a caffeine bug?

The Hidden Richness

In depths of brown, there's treasure hid,
Just beneath the foamy lid.
A sprinkle of joy, a shot of glee,
Oh, the things my coffee sees!

Each sip a puzzle, clinks and clinks,
As I sip, I pause, and think.
Is there magic in this brew?
Or am I just a pea-brained fool?

The coffee's warmth, a hug so nice,
Reflecting on life's strange advice.
Do beans have dreams like you and me?
Or just froth and destiny?

In my cup, the answers stir,
As I consider life's little blur.
Pour me another, let's dig deep,
There's wealth in sips that we can keep!

A Sip of Serenity

With every sip, I'm on a quest,
For mocha magic and a moment's rest.
Do I find peace or just a buzz?
In this bitter drink, what truly was?

A little latte art, a heart so fine,
Brewing storms while I sip divine.
Is life just foam, or something more?
With each caress, it starts to soar.

The world slows down, a comic scene,
As I ponder beans of evergreen.
I chuckle softly, the vibe is right,
Caffeine and smiles, such sweet delight!

So here's to mugs that bring us glee,
In every drop, a jubilee.
Stirring thoughts within the steam,
Oh what a funny little dream!

The Search Beneath the Surface

In a mug so bold and round,
Questions swirl, yet none are found.
Where's the wisdom? Where's the cheer?
Perhaps it's hiding, oh so near.

Sipping slowly, I take a pause,
Did I notice the foam's applause?
A sprinkle of joy atop the brew,
Lost in thoughts of caffeine stew.

Zooming in, the patterns dance,
A latte art of fate's romance.
Is life's meaning in the steam?
Or is it just a caffeine dream?

With every gulp, I ponder wide,
Is wit contained inside the tide?
My cup may reveal more than it seems,
Just a sip, to spark wild dreams.

Whispers of Liquid Warmth.

In the morning, with cup held tight,
I find my joy, my sheer delight.
What secrets lie in this dark brew?
Maybe it knows more than I do!

A swirl, a slosh, it gently sighs,
Could coffee be the wisest guise?
I lean in close, hear whispers low,
"Just drink me up, and let it flow!"

Each sip a chuckle, bittersweet,
Life's riddles hidden in this treat.
I grin, concoct absurdity,
As flavors merge in pure flattery.

With every ounce that warms my soul,
I ponder if it's making me whole.
But for now, I'll keep the jest,
Finding joy in each caffeine quest.

Brewed Reflections

Peering deep into my cup,
What fortune lurks, what dreams erupt?
A swirl of caramel, a hint of gloom,
Or is that just this morning's doom?

I take a sip, it tickles my mind,
Thoughts percolate, undefined.
Perhaps the answer's in this blend,
Or just a sugar rush I suspend.

My coffee's hot, yet questions freeze,
Does it hold solutions, if you please?
Laughter bubbles in every swirl,
As I contemplate this caffeinated whirl.

With laughter strong, I raise my cup,
Can it really lift me up?
In this brew, is life's grand scheme?
Or just a frothy, foamy dream?

The Elixir of Insight

This potion dark, it fuels my day,
With every sip, my worries sway.
Wisdom brewed, or just the jitters?
Chatting with steam, leaving me in twitters.

I lift the cup, a sacred rite,
What sage advice awaits this bite?
Caffeine calls me, "Join the fun!
Unravel life before it's done!"

The dregs reveal a tale or two,
Of far-off lands and skies so blue.
Or just my brain, in hyperdrive,
Inventing stories to survive.

Each gulp a giggle, each drop a jest,
What can be better than this quest?
To sip and ponder, laugh, and dream,
In coffee's hug, we plot and scheme.

An Ode to Morning Brews

Steam rises high, like dreams take flight,
The bitter splash brightens the soft daylight.
Sipping my potion, the world's my stage,
In this cup of warmth, I share my age.

The spoon does a dance, swirling around,
As I ponder the ways my brain can be found.
Should I add sugar or stick with the cream?
In this caffeinated world, I'm living the dream.

Brewed Moments

In the morning rush, my cup cries out,
'Fill me up quick, or face the pout!'
Java jitters brew laughter and cheer,
Fueling my chaos while I fight off fear.

Every sip brings thoughts that make me grin,
Silly reflections, where do I begin?
Do I want espresso or a latte twist?
In this brew of life, I'll add to my list.

The Alchemy of a Mug

A splash here, a splash there, what's that aroma?
Turning plain water into liquid euphoria.
Bubbles of laughter dance on my lip,
With each tiny sip, reality's skip.

Oh, frothy delight, my daily surprise,
Blending ground beans in morning skies.
I find my muse in the steam that swirls,
As the universe giggles, and my thoughts unfurl.

Sugary Philosophy

Caffeine and sugar are partners in crime,
Creating deep thoughts, one sip at a time.
'What's the meaning?' I ponder with glee,
While my cup laughs back, 'Just enjoy me!'

Stirring the sweetness, I muse and I sigh,
Pouring my hopes like clouds passing by.
Life's a puzzle, or maybe a cake,
With coffee as glue, we mold and we make.

Dialogues in a Demitasse

In the tiny cup of fate, I sip,
Dreams and grounds swirl, take a trip.
Conversations with a caffeine muse,
My sleepy brain, in laughs, will choose.

A swirl of foam, like thoughts afloat,
Biscuit crumbs dance, a light-hearted quote.
"Am I awake?" I ask the brew,
It chuckles back, "A sip or two?"

With every drop, a riddle brews,
I debate with shadows, odd and profuse.
Laughter rises, steam escapes,
In this small cup, I craft my shapes.

So here I sit, absurdly wise,
In a mere demitasse, less the guise.
For coffee's truth is plain to see,
Life's better shared with a brew and glee.

Late Night Beans of Wisdom

When the clock strikes three, I brew a pot,
Midnight confessions, oh, coffee, you've got.
Staring at beans, my mind's a whirl,
This late-night source unveils a pearl.

Cup in hand, I ponder the stars,
Each sip brings tales from Venus to Mars.
Do they laugh at us, those distant lights?
Or drip their dreams into earthly nights?

"Why so bitter?" I question the blend,
"Because life's a joke," the dark roast will send.
A chuckle escapes, as I gleefully sip,
In a mug's embrace, philosophy takes a trip.

So here I sit, night's giddy surprise,
With beans as my guides, I sip, I rise.
In jests of flavor, I find my muse,
Late night wisdom, oh dear, I'll never lose!

Awakening Whispers

Morning yawns, the kettle sings,
Steam rises high, like hopeful wings.
The mug calls out, "Come have a taste,"
In this warm hug, the day's embraced.

Whispers swirl in the fragrant air,
Spoon clinks softly, what's waiting there?
Each sip reveals a giggly grin,
Life's silliness, where to begin?

"Is this life?" I ask the frothy foam,
"Nonsense!" it answers, "Just feel at home."
With every gulp, the chaos cheers,
Funny paradoxes chase off the fears.

So here I stand, with laughter bright,
In this ceramic vessel, I find delight.
A cup of joy, not too deep or dark,
Awakening whispers, coffee's spark.

Paradox in a Porcelain Cup

In a porcelain shell, I dive headfirst,
Bubbles of laughter, a caffeine burst.
Sweetness mingles with a bitter bite,
Life's curious dance, oh, what a sight!

"Why can't I fly?" I glare in the brew,
The cup just laughs, "Not much you can do."
Caffeine humor spills over the rim,
Life's absurdities never grow dim.

With each little sip, I ponder and grin,
Caught in this trap where nonsense wears thin.
"What's next?" I slurp, the cup can't reply,
Yet here I am, with dreams that can fly.

A paradox here, in sips we find,
The joy in folly, the chaos aligned.
So I raise my mug, a toast to this game,
In porcelain truth, life's fun will remain.

Captured Essence

In a mug so dark and deep,
I ponder life while half-asleep.
With frothy swirls and caffeine dreams,
I sip my way through silly schemes.

The beans conspire, they giggle too,
Every drop a joke, who knew?
A latte art that starts to dance,
Inviting me to take a chance.

Oh, the dreams that swirl and whip,
With every gulp, I try not to trip.
A sip of hope, a dash of fun,
This comedy in a cup undone.

So cheers to brews, and laughter's claim,
Each cup a chuckle, none the same.
I raise my mug, in jest I wait,
For life's next punchline to relate.

A Journey in the Java

A steaming cup takes me away,
To lands where beans just laugh and play.
I'll journey through each fragrant town,
With coffee cheers, I'll never frown.

The barista's wink, a playful jest,
Pouring dreams in every fest.
Espresso shots like fireworks pop,
With every drink, I hop, hop, hop.

From drip to French, it's quite a ride,
On caffeine waves, I take my stride.
I'll barrel roll in mocha streams,
While frothy mounds fuel silly dreams.

So here's to java's joyful spree,
Each slurp, a dance, invigorates me.
A comic tour in every brew,
This cup of cheer, my point of view.

Bubbles of Introspection

Tiny bubbles rise with glee,
In my coffee, they speak to me.
They giggle soft, they swirl around,
With bubbly thoughts, a cheerful sound.

Each sip a laugh, a playful push,
As frothy caps make my heart mush.
A cappuccino's witty grin,
Invites the fun to bubble in.

In every gulp, a riddle shines,
What's the secret in these lines?
Is it cream or sugar's tease,
That humors me and grants me peace?

So let's not fret, let's take a chance,
In coffee's world, we laugh and dance.
With every sip, a chuckle's born,
Through foamy fun, I'm never worn.

Awakening Within the Espresso

This tiny shot, a liquid spark,
Awakens joy; it hits the mark.
In every sip, there's wonder found,
A jolt of laughter, giggles abound.

A dance of beans in heated court,
As swirling steam brings humor's fort.
The cup, a stage for frothy shows,
With smiles that bloom as caffeine flows.

I take a sip, the world is bright,
A comic twist, pure delight.
The espresso whispers, 'Join my fun!'
And in that moment, laughs are spun.

So raise a cup to morning cheer,
In every brew, absurdity's near.
We'll toast to life, one sip at a time,
With coffee's jests, oh how they rhyme!

A Quiet Brew's Whisper

In the morning light, I pour,
A java potion, I adore.
Tiny beans with tales to tell,
A frothy mug, my cozy spell.

As steam curls up into the air,
I ponder life without a care.
Chocolate swirls, a dance so sweet,
Hey, is that a song from my old feet?

Each sip a clock, it ticks away,
I laugh at dreams that roam and play.
With every gulp, I surf the tide,
Of caffeinated thoughts inside.

The cream cascades, a frothy sight,
Who knew my cup held such delight?
A carousel of thoughts takes flight,
In this café, I'm taking flight.

Aroma of Intentions

In a porcelain sea, I drift and sip,
Intentions float, on the edge, they slip.
Chocolate or vanilla, which to choose?
Oh, the paradox of daily brews!

The strong, the bold, they make me swoon,
While cappuccino calls like a morning tune.
Just a splash, a sprinkle, oh so wise,
These little cups hold vast surprise.

In every drop, a wrinkled fate,
Espresso shots can fix a state.
A twist of fate in every blend,
Or maybe just a trend to mend?

So I smile, it warms my soul,
This liquid love that makes me whole.
With every laugh and every sigh,
My coffee cup knows how to tie.

Heartfelt Grounds

At the bottom of my cup, I see,
A whirlpool of dreams, come dance with me.
Coffee grounds with ancient lore,
Each slurp reveals what's in store.

A frothy heart with mischief beats,
I sip and ponder my morning feats.
Did I send that text? Or was it lost?
Such is the price of my caffeine cost!

The barista winks, my secrets found,
As laughter bubbles, a joyful sound.
In this café, I'm oddly blessed,
Life's quirky humor I must digest.

A dash of milk, a splash of cheer,
Mismatched socks, no doubts, no fear.
This cup of warmth, a friend indeed,
With every sip, it plants a seed.

Bitter Tales and Sweet Dreams

A mug of darkness sitting wide,
Swirls of chaos I can't abide.
Do I swap tales with the creamer,
Or have I gone just a bit greener?

Bitter sips from the morning grind,
Laughter lurks, you will find.
I chase the steam like a playful ghost,
In the world of brews, I almost boast.

The coffee shop, my comedy stage,
Each latte art, a new page.
As jokes brew thick, the flavors blend,
In caffeine's arms, I find my friend.

So here's to spills and coffee stains,
The laughter echoes, yet remains.
With each sweet sip, I feel alive,
In bitter tales, my dreams do thrive.

Trails of Steam and Thought

In morning's light, a brew so fine,
A dance of steam, my daily sign.
The cup does whisper, secrets sweet,
Of puddled dreams and hurried feet.

With every sip, a giggle grows,
Is that my boss or just a prose?
My thoughts swirl round like frothy cream,
In this dark brew, I lose my dream.

A jolt of joy, a caffeinated cheer,
Hope that today, I won't disappear.
Espresso shots, like tiny bells,
Ring out tales that caffeine tells.

Yet, when I spill, I laugh it off,
My shirt's a canvas, not a scoff.
The stains of life, a messy art,
In coffee's grip, I've found my heart.

Poured Perspectives

With every pour, a new view forms,
A latte swirl that dodges norms.
Espressos call, like sirens' cries,
I raise my cup to cloudy skies.

I ponder tales of beans and brew,
What's bitter truth, what's sweet and true?
A splash of milk gives me some grace,
As foamy cap, I find my place.

Oh, coffee grounds, my past laid bare,
In every sip, a joke to share.
They swirl and dance, a circus show,
With every gulp, my worries go.

The world spins fast, I sip and chill,
A punch of caffeine with a likely thrill.
I laugh at life, so absurdly bright,
Like sugar sprinkles on a midnight flight.

The Quiet Companion

In quiet mornings, just me and brew,
A steaming friend that knows my view.
As silence wraps, the kettle sings,
With every sip, my heart takes wings.

The spoon clinks soft, a gentle tune,
Caffeine winks like a cheeky moon.
I ponder life 'neath froth's embrace,
In porcelain peace, I find my space.

I try to solve my puzzles here,
But coffee laughs, "Oh dear, oh dear!"
With each warm gulp, wisdom unfolds,
Yet still, I spill my dreams, it holds.

A quiet murmur, my soul's refrain,
In every drop, joy turns to gain.
Though cups may empty, I'll refill soon,
In steam and stillness, I find my tune.

The Perfect Blend of Silence

In cozy corners, sipping slow,
A blend of thoughts, like coffee flow.
The world outside can hustle fast,
But here in silence, I'll make it last.

With darkened shades and muffin crumbs,
I ponder worlds, war, and drums.
Each cup a passport, each sip a flight,
Through frothy clouds, oh what delight!

Amid the drips and distant chats,
I chase the fables of coffee rats.
They tell me tales of beans and pride,
In every sip, a world to ride.

Oh, perfect blend, you know my heart,
With each warm hug, you play your part.
Together we share a silly dance,
In every brew, I take a chance.

A Dark Roast Revelations

In the depths of that black brew,
I ponder life, yes, it's true.
The grounds whisper secrets, oh so bold,
Of mysteries that never grow old.

The milk froths with laughter, it spills,
As I sip away all my morning ills.
A swirl of sugar, a dash of cheer,
Turns my frown into a grin, I shed a tear.

Stirring thoughts like a barista's craft,
The espresso shot lifts my spirits, what a laugh!
Each sip a joke, a giggle shared,
In this cup of magic, I'm unprepared.

Yet still, I ponder, what's brewing next?
Beyond the foam, life feels perplexed.
A dark roast dilemma, laughter's disguise,
In every sip, I find quirky surprise.

Conversations with the Cup

I sit and chat with my trusty mug,
It spills the gossip, gives me a shrug.
The coffee's hot, but the jokes are cold,
A tale of beans that never gets old.

"Why so bitter?" I tease with a grin,
It bubbles back, "It's the grind within!"
A saucer sidekick, in this laugh parade,
Together we brew the perfect charade.

As I sip smartly, it starts to confess,
"With every splash, I aim to impress!"
The swirl of caffeine is a comic breeze,
With every gulp, I take life with ease.

A caffeine chat, it's quite absurd,
The wisdom of trees, in every stirred word.
It knows my dreams, my plans and my fears,
Over steaming waters, we share hearty cheers!

Bitter Truths, Sweet Discoveries

In the depths, a bitter truth hides,
Like the coffee grounds beneath these tides.
But with every sip, the sweetness leaps,
A contradiction that giggles and creeps.

"Life's like this mug," I jest with a wink,
"Pour in your dreams, give them a think!"
A frothy swirl chimes in with a smirk,
"Do you want cream, or a bit of that quirk?"

The contrast enchants, it's all in the blend,
Each slosh of coffee, a twist and a bend.
I guffaw at life's many flavors and woes,
In every cup lies a tale that just flows.

So here's to the bitter, the sweet, and the zest,
In this cup of laughter, I find my best.
Each sip brings a chuckle, a reason to cheer,
In the cafe of dreams, there's nothing to fear!

Sweet Discoveries

In a mocha mix, discoveries bloom,
Sugary sweetness, in my cozy room.
With every drop, a revelation stirs,
Like the funny chatter of drifting birds.

Chocolate whispers while the milk pirouettes,
It's a waltz of flavors, no regrets!
I catch a chuckle in the steam that swirls,
My heart leaps high, as sweetness unfurls.

The caramel smiles with a golden hue,
"What secrets do you hold, oh chai brew?"
A sip of joy, in laughter we bask,
This cup of cheer, my daily task!

So here's to the wonders that live in each swig,
Where laughter dances, and worries grow big.
A latte of life with sprinkles of fun,
In every brew, find joy in the run.

In the Wake of the Steam

The steam rises, like thoughts on the fly,
I laugh at the whispers that tickle the sky.
"Why is it hot?" I muse with delight,
As the coffee giggles, "We're warming the night!"

In the swirl of the cup, there's a party of foam,
Each bubble a story, a giggle, a poem.
Pour on the milk like a painter's grand brush,
The palette of flavors ignites in a rush.

I sip on the warmth, it sparks up a grin,
"Is there wisdom in coffee?" I ask with a spin.
It chuckles back softly, "You'll find it in time,
In the froth and the drip, life's laughter's the rhyme."

So I ponder the mysteries, one sip at a time,
In a cup of delight, where the jokes always climb.
As the last drop escapes, I savor the cheer,
This steaming adventure keeps life full of cheer!

Frosted Moments in a Warm Embrace

In the froth, I see my fate,
A heart-shaped shape, oh, isn't that great?
Marshmallows dancing, oh what a sight,
Sipping my dreams in the morning light.

The mug sings songs of past spills,
Of sugar highs and caffeine thrills,
With every gulp, my worries wane,
A cocoa cloud meets my brain's train.

This steaming cup, a wondrous friend,
To frosty mornings that never end,
Laughter bubbles, stories blend,
In this cup, I find my mend.

With cinnamon swirls and starlit glee,
Coffee art that's just for me,
In each sip, a giggle awaits,
Life feels grand; I must celebrate!

Café Chronicles

In a little cup, my tales unfold,
With every sip, secrets told,
The barista winks, what's the dare?
Espresso shots—ah, I declare!

Sipping dreams that dance with cream,
In this haven, I plot and scheme,
Chatting with strangers, laughter flows,
Caffeine unites us—who really knows?

Muffins crumble, oh what a mess!
Yet here we linger, I must confess,
With pastries warm and coffee hot,
Life's tales are brewed, while we share thoughts.

In frothy cups, adventures thrive,
Where legends brew and ideas strive,
Take a seat; let wonders brew,
The café buzz is just for you!

A Quest in Every Sip

With every cup, a quest begins,
Chasing flavors, sipping whims,
Frothy lands of mocha delight,
A journey sparked, oh what a bite!

My spoon's a sword, my cup, a shield,
In this world where dreams are revealed,
Espresso elves, they spill the lore,
Of secret blends behind each door.

Latte lakes, caramel hills,
Adventure brews with quirky thrills,
With chocolate rivers flowing near,
Each sip uncovers paths unclear.

In every taste, a giggle hides,
We navigate on coffee tides,
Sip-wise heroes, we rise and take,
On a quest where friendships make!

Beyond the Brew

Beyond the brew, there's magic steeped,
With every sip, a promise leaped,
Whispers floating, jokes on cookies,
My coffee talks—no need for bookies!

Grains of laughter filter through,
In strange concoctions, dreams renew,
Oh, what spices stir in here?
A potion brewed to vanquish fear!

Slurp and snicker, cheers abound,
In this dark elixir, joy is found,
With each frothy wave, problems fade,
Life's a comedy, perfectly made!

So let's toast to cups held high,
With frothy crowns beneath the sky,
In every droplet, a silly tale,
In this wonderfully caffeinated gale!

Echoes of Yesterday in Every Sip

Waking up with dreams so steep,
A jolt of joy, I take a leap.
The swirling foams, a playful tease,
In every sip, the past just flees.

A memory of a cake once baked,
Chocolate crumbs, oh, how they flaked.
With laughter brewed in every cup,
I chase the thoughts that bubble up.

A splash of cream, a drizzle fine,
This liquid bliss, divine design.
Yet each sip whispers tales untold,
With every gulp, my secrets sold.

So raise your mug to moments bold,
In laughter's grip, and tales retold.
Each cup, a riddle, how absurd!
The answers lie where coffee swirled.

A Journey Through Grounds

From bean to brew, I take a ride,
With every sip, my thoughts collide.
The grounds beneath, they swirl and dance,
In caffeine's grip, I find my chance.

A dash of sugar, a pinch of fun,
Stirring chaos, just begun.
I ponder life in frothy waves,
Each gulp a quest that misbehaves.

The coffee shop's my goofy stage,
Where every sip ignites my rage.
A latte art that's meant to charm,
Hides secrets vague, yet packed with balm.

Adventures brewed in mugs of cheer,
You never know what's hiding near.
So let's toast to the daily grind,
In every cup, what will we find?

Comfort and Conundrum

In a cozy mug, confusion brews,
With every sip, the doubt renews.
A swirl of cream, a sprinkle bright,
Is it solace or a fright tonight?

Sipping slow, the steam does wind,
What answers lurk? I'm feeling blind.
The coffee's warmth, a soft embrace,
Yet trouble brews at a frenzied pace.

A dash of humor in every roast,
I laugh at what I love the most.
Am I a knight or just a fool?
In coffee's kingdom, I play the rule.

So pass me beans, the darkest roast,
In this café, I'm now the host.
Each cup a puzzle, every drop,
A comedy where worries stop.

The Heart of the Brew

A fragrant cloud in morning light,
I dive in deep, a silly fight.
With every sip, my mind's a dance,
The coffee's warmth my constant trance.

A filter full of thoughts and dreams,
I stir my heart in frothy themes.
What's life's goal? I sip and ponder,
In every gulp, I drift and wander.

The café's buzz, a joyful hum,
All my questions, where are they from?
With laughter mixed like cream and milk,
Each drop brings comfort, soft as silk.

So here I am, mug held high,
With every gulp, I flirt and sigh.
In this warm brew, I feel alive,
With coffee's charm, I thrive and strive.

Steam Rising

In the morning light, the mug does gleam,
The brew inside, oh how it seems!
A splash of joy, a swirl of hope,
Determined spirits start to cope.

Sipping slow, the warmth extends,
With each sip, my sanity mends.
I ponder life's great mystery,
Like how to make toast without a history.

Coffee's aroma brings witty dreams,
Of far-off lands and chocolate creams.
Each sip a riddle, each gulp a jest,
I swear this cup knows me the best!

So here's to brews that tease and play,
Turning mundane to a lucky day.
With frothy mustaches, we caffeinate,
And giggle loudly at our fate.

Dreams Unfold

Pour it hot, a magic brew,
With every swirl, my wish comes true.
Creamy layers bring forth a smile,
Awakening dreams that beguile.

Dancing swirls like a circus show,
Turns my woes to a fun-filled glow.
As the spoon clinks in witty tune,
This cup's a jester, my morning boon.

With every sip, I take a whim,
The world seems bright, the lights don't dim.
A latte's giggle, a coffee's wink,
Who knew hot beans could make one think?

So join me here, let's find a pun,
In every sip, let laughter run.
A mug of cheer in every blend,
Coffee's the clarity I commend.

Awakening in a Coffee Ring

A circle of joy, a spill of cheer,
In each coffee ring, the day is near.
Let's gather clues from the darkened grounds,
To solve the mysteries and laugh all 'round!

Flecks of java like sprinkled fate,
Telling tales of a caffeinated state.
Lost in flavors, I plot and scheme,
Is there cappuccino in every dream?

Giggles float like espresso foam,
Adding fun to the boring tome.
With chocolate sprinkles, we'll join the fun,
In sips of joy, our worries shun.

Each ring a map of jests and quotes,
Navigating life in caffeinated boats.
So raise your cup, let laughter cling,
To each coffee circle, let our hearts sing!

A Sip of Solace

In the depths of my coffee cup,
I find a world that lifts me up.
Each warm embrace, a secret told,
With a giggle shared, and laughter bold.

One sip in, I'm a sage of sorts,
With mugs as my magic and grace that resorts.
The drippings dance like notes on air,
In every swirl, life becomes fair.

Caramel whispers, hints of glee,
As I contemplate the universe with glee.
Coffee beans have stories to weave,
Creating laughter that we believe.

So here's to brews that light our path,
With tasty twists and plenty of math.
Each cup a riddle, with joy adorned,
In every sip, life's humor is born!

Unwritten Stories in Each Drip

As droplets fall, tales come alive,
Hidden whispers that make us thrive.
Each drip a secret, each pause a grin,
Stirring the heartbeats from within.

A coffee saga with frothy plots,
We'll write our jokes, forget the knots.
With every pour, the humor flows,
Unwritten stories the cup bestows.

Brewed adventures in ceramic charms,
Tales of joy held in liquid arms.
From bitter to sweet, and back again,
This jester's cup brings laughter's reign.

So lift your mugs, let's toast to fate,
In this steaming circus, we celebrate.
For every sip is a wink to bring,
The best of laughs in a world to sing!

In the Wake of the Pour

In the morning light, I stumble near,
With a mug that's whispering thoughts sincere.
Is it the cream or the beans that I crave?
So many questions, yet I still misbehave.

Steam rises up like my hopes in the day,
Will I find wisdom or just a good spray?
I sip and I ponder, my brain needs a tune,
Perhaps life's answers brew best with a spoon.

A dash of confusion, a sprinkle of zest,
This cup has my heart, it's a love that won't rest.
As I swish 'round the cup, I peer deep within,
Is it a latte I ponder or where to begin?

Each drop tells a story, each swirl holds a jest,
In thick foamy layers, I'm feeling quite blessed.
So I pour out my worries, oh where did they go?
In a cup filled with laughter, I'm starting to flow.

Shadows in the Latte

In the swirl of my brew, I see shadows dance,
A frothy disguise, oh isn't it a chance?
What secrets they hide in their milky white foam,
Could they solve riddles of life, or feel like home?

The spoon stirs my dreams, with a clink and a cheer,
Maybe a sip will banish my fear.
Laughter bubbles up, in this caffeinated plight,
As I wonder if they hold clues to my plight.

With each slurp and giggle, my troubles disperse,
Is it just caffeine, or can it heal the universe?
Tales of jittery journeys they dare to unfurl,
In a cup of enchantment, I twirl and I whirl.

The shadows are sly, they giggle and tease,
Is it coffee who plays, or me who's a breeze?
With each little sip, the day seems less murky,
I toast to my thoughts—cheers, dear old jerky!

Caffeine and Contemplation

In a cup of brown magic, I ponder my fate,
Coffee grounds whisper, "Don't make haste, mate."
Do beans really bear the weight of my dreams?
Or is the real answer just sugar and creams?

A sip of this potion ignites every thought,
Does chaos emerge or clarity sought?
Oh, the puns of the barista, they crack me each morn,
"Can I coffee to you?" and I'm hopelessly sworn.

Between sips and snorts, thoughts bubble on up,
Shaped like a heart, or maybe a pup?
As froth spills like secrets, and laughter is bold,
The warmth in my hands tells stories untold.

Caffeine's a muse, a help or a fright,
Should I chase after dreams or just sip with delight?
With each playful gulp, I wonder if I'll see,
Does the brew brew wisdom, or just energize me?

The Soul in a Steaming Cup

Beneath the steam curls, does fortune abide?
Or is it just coffee trying to hide?
I cradle my cup like it's holding a code,
A map to my joy in this caffeinated ode.

Stirring the cosmos with a flick of my spoon,
Can I brew a solution by afternoon?
Each sip's a new chapter, a riddle, a play,
Would my woes dissolve if I just dared to stay?

A dance with the foam, oh, a swirling delight,
Do these flavors unlock the mysteries of night?
With flavors and giggles, their essence adorned,
Is my soul just as lively or slightly less scorned?

Oh, fragrant elixir, let the silliness flow,
In this comedy cup, I find laughter to grow.
So here's to the chaos, the laughter, the fun,
In the soul of my cup, I think I have won!

In Search of the Missing Cream

I poured it hot, I poured it fast,
But where's the cream? It's a brew-blast!
My cup of joy is now a plight,
Just me, my beans, and this dark night.

I shake the fridge, I check the shelf,
It's vanished like my former self!
Swirls of brown turn me a-beam,
Oh, life's a joke without that cream!

I laugh at my milky catastrophe,
A comedy of errors, oh so crafty!
With every sip, I feel the scream,
Of coffee's truth without that cream.

Perhaps, in life, we're like this mug,
Searching for warmth, or just a hug!
So here I sip, with whimsy beams,
In this wild game of missing creams.

Sweetness and Shadows

A splash of syrup, a dash of fun,
Yet bitter sips say it's never done.
I look for sugar, where could it flee?
A sweet escape? Nah, just lost keys!

The shadows linger, they mock my taste,
Each sip I take feels like a waste.
"More sweetness please!" my heart does cry,
But the cup just glares, like a judgmental eye.

Do donuts know of my caffeinated quest?
To find the sweet and dodge the jest?
So I sip and ponder with a grin,
Maybe my search is where sweetness begins!

At the bottom, I find a lost smudge,
A relic of sugar, a long-held grudge.
Life's full of flavors, a wild frolic,
So bring me the sweet over just a tonic!

Musings in a Mocha

In my mocha wonder, I dive so deep,
What secrets lie in this warm, sweet heap?
Froth on the surface, oh so divine,
But within the cup, is leisure a sign?

A dance of chocolate, so rich and bold,
Yet am I sipping or just getting old?
This liquid bliss, a temporary friend,
While I ponder if there's more 'round the bend.

Sipping slowly, I catch a grin,
Life's creamy moments are where to begin.
Each gulp a puzzle, each swirl a clue,
As I laugh with my mocha, my old buddy brew.

In the end, I toast with delight,
For all the weird thoughts in the dead of night.
Mocha dreams and giggles blend,
Tomorrow's cup, a new sip, a new trend!

The Aroma of Unanswered Questions

I wake each morn to brewing air,
Hints of jokes and funny hair.
The kettle sings, but what's the score?
Am I doing life right? Who knows anymore?

Coffee swirls with dreams inside,
Questions bounce while I ride this tide.
"The beans are strong, what's brewing next?"
I raise my mug, perplexed, perplexed!

A sip of laughter, a dash of fright,
The aroma whispers in morning light.
"Did I add the cream? Or just my fears?"
In thoughts that linger, I drown in cheers!

So here's to brews steeped in doubt,
A blend of giggles that life's about.
With every scent, I embrace the plight,
Of coffee dreams, that bring such delight!

Aroma of Ambivalence

In the mug, a dark affair,
A swirl of dreams and grocery fare,
I ponder life with every sip,
Is it wisdom or just a caffeine trip?

Steam rises like my thoughts on high,
Am I awake or just asking why?
With each gulp, a giggling dance,
Is coffee fortune, or a caffeine trance?

The world spins mad in a caffeine haze,
I ponder existence in swirling maze,
With sugar and cream, I'm finding bliss,
Or just a brew that's hard to miss?

So here's to the cup that keeps me guessing,
A liquid riddle that's quite arresting,
Each drop, a chuckle, a silly little dream,
That life's a frothy cappuccino theme.

The Mysterious Blend

A blend of beans, a twist of fate,
Mysteries stir in a caffeinated state,
I sip and wonder, what's this mix?
Is it magic or just clever tricks?

Barista grins, a cryptic wink,
With every sip, I rethink my drink,
Am I drinking joy or just a brew?
A frothy answer, cloudy and blue?

Espresso whispers secrets so deep,
While I juggle thoughts, in caffeinated sleep,
With laughter bubbling at the cup's rim,
Is this my life or a caffeine whim?

Oh, cup of chaos, what do you hold?
A story of warmth, or tales of old?
In every gulp, I giggle and blink,
Perhaps it's me that needs a rethink.

Caffeine and Contemplation

A swirl of doubts in my morning brew,
Are they real, or just thoughts askew?
With each bold sip, I weigh the cost,
Of daydreams brewed and laughter tossed.

I ponder life with a latte swirl,
Thoughts rolling 'round like legs of a pearl,
With froth and foam, I entertain,
Is meaning here or lost in the grain?

Each slurp a journey, a flight of cheer,
What happened to my plans for the year?
Am I wiser now, or just wired more?
Caffeine's my muse, oh what's in store?

Sips of sanity, laughs in between,
In every cup, I find the unseen,
So raise your mugs, let's toast to this,
A caffeinated quest, a humorous bliss.

Serenity in a Soupy Swirl

In the depths of a cup, a calm so bright,
Like clouds soft dancing in soft daylight,
A soupy swirl of hope and glee,
With every sip, I long to be free.

The spoon comes alive, with a playful spin,
Chasing thoughts that giggle within,
Is this tranquility or just a tease?
Or just a mug that won't give me peace?

A dash of cinnamon, a sprinkle of fun,
With steam rising high, our jests have just begun,
I slurp and smile, a whimsical thrill,
Is it coffee or just time standing still?

So here's my mug, a whimsical brew,
In every sip, I find something new,
In this liquid hug, life's silliness swirls,
Serenity served in playful curls.

Brewed Reflections

In the morning light I stand,
With mug in hand, it's quite the bland.
Each sip reveals a little truth,
Or maybe just my quest for sleuth.

The cream swirls like my thoughts today,
A caffeinated game I play.
Do I ponder life's big plot?
Or just the fact it's tasting hot?

Each drip of joy, a tiny laugh,
A sugar cube, my other half.
The beans conspire, they hold a tale,
Of dreams that foam, then softly fail.

With every gulp, I find my muse,
Do I want coffee or wine to choose?
In this mug, my worries fade,
But will this buzz just leave me swayed?

The Essence of Morning

The rooster crows, it starts anew,
But I'm awake with coffee brew.
The rich aroma calls my name,
Yet I down it like it's a game.

I sip and swirl, a caffeinated dance,
This cup's my partner in a trance.
Is it the brew or the mug's delight?
Funny how it makes wrongs feel right.

Each bubble pops, a laugh it sends,
A perfect drink where time transcends.
Can I find wisdom in a grind?
Or is it just beans that I find?

I raise my cup, to all it brings,
A dose of cheer and silly things.
In every drop, a giggle hides,
With coffee, joy and humor rides.

Sips of Solitude

Alone I sit, my trusty brew,
A world of thoughts, just me and you.
With steam that twirls like thoughts aflight,
This cup holds dreams that shine so bright.

I ponder laughter, frowns and grins,
As coffee spills where chaos spins.
Do I drink deep or take it slow?
Who knew the cup would steal the show?

With chocolate sprinkles on the top,
I take a sip, then let out a pop.
Life's peculiar when faced with foam,
Is this my heart? Just froth? My home?

In solitude I find it clear,
Sips of joy, sprinkle of cheer.
The world outside may fade away,
But inside this cup, I choose to stay.

In the Depths of Java

In Java's depths, I dive and swim,
With every sip, my thoughts grow slim.
Is caffeine magic, or am I mad?
In this brown ocean, I feel both glad.

Drowned in flavor, dark and bold,
A secret world begins to unfold.
Can coffee beans unlock the door?
Or just another way to want more?

A whirl of cream, a splash of fun,
Together we bask in the morning sun.
Is it the jitters or the giggles?
I swear I hear my mug do wiggles!

Life's absurd, but here I find,
In every gulp, a truth aligned.
With a chuckle and a slurp, I say,
Today's my cup, come what may!

Deep Brews and Deeper Thoughts

In the morning light, I sip my brew,
The chatter of beans, like whispers, ensue.
Each drop a riddle, warm and so bright,
What's life's great secret? My cup holds it tight.

With each slurp I ponder, should I add cream?
Or just take it black, like a loner's old dream?
I chuckle to think, it's just roast in a cup,
Yet here I am, trying to figure it up.

My mug smiles back, it knows me too well,
A liquid companion, oh how we gel!
But today it's hot, almost burning my tongue,
So deep in my thoughts, I'm still feeling young.

With swirling aromas that dance in the air,
I muse about life while pretending to care.
A few sips of joy in this ceramic throne,
Maybe it's wisdom, or caffeine on loan.

Whispers in the Wake

The kettle sings softly, a lullaby sweet,
As I ponder the lives in my morning retreat.
Steam swirls like dreams, elusive and bold,
In search of a tale, or perhaps just some gold.

Sip after sip, my thoughts float and sway,
What do coffee beans think of our day?
Do they plot their revenge or seek to delight?
Or are they just beans, growing chill in the night?

A dance of the spoon in the sugar's embrace,
Oh, how can a drink bring such joy to my face?
Between buds and brews, I giggle and muse,
In a cup full of laughter, life's best kind of fuse.

I take one last gulp, and I'm ready to go,
A philosopher brewed in my nine-ounce show.
Cheerful concoctions, the hearty, the bold,
Each sip a reminder, that life's hard to hold.

The Dance of Milk and Sugar

Creamer pirouettes, sweet sugar takes flight,
Like a ballet of flavors, a morning delight.
Every swirl a giggle, a frothy charade,
This cup is a canvas, my hunger on parade.

I wonder if coffee is just a facade,
Pouring out wisdom, while being a fraud.
Its dark, brooding whispers, a clever charmer,
Promising clarity, but brewing just drama.

In the clatter of cups, there's laughter to chase,
As I sip from my mug, I find my own pace.
With each silly thought, I expand and I grow,
Like froth on my latte, I steal the show.

Oh, what a concoction of joy in my brew,
My cup of sweet joy, a chaos I knew.
So laugh with me now, as I dance with my cup,
In this circus of life, let's giggle it up!

Unraveling Beneath the Foam

A fortress of foam sits atop my warm drink,
What mysteries lie there? I pause and I think.
Underneath the froth, real stories reside,
Is it caffeine magic or just the joy ride?

I gaze at the swirls, a canvas of the day,
What's brewed in this cup? Oh, where do I stray?
Each bubble, a secret, or maybe just air,
A giggle escapes as I sip without care.

As cream meets the coffee, a meeting of minds,
Their dance is absurd, what fun it all finds!
Perhaps life's a blend of mishaps and cheer,
With flavors so rich, let's all toast to beer?

In search of the truth that the beans have concealed,
With a hearty guffaw, yet the mystery healed.
So raise up your mugs, let's toast to the brew,
For laughter's the meaning in coffee anew!

Savoring the Solitary

Alone with my mug, glance at the wall,
It stares back at me, silence enthralls.
The steam plays a dance, like it knows my fate,
Is it my coffee or just a long wait?

A sip and a giggle, it feels quite absurd,
It whispers my secrets, not saying a word.
I ponder the depths of dark, swirling glee,
Is this mug got the answers, or just caffeine?

While stirring my thoughts, I take in the scene,
Spilled sugar the proof of my caffeine dream.
The jitter, the chuckle, my heart starts to race,
Who knew my morning would turn into space?

So here's to the moments, both silly and bright,
In the depths of my cup, I find sheer delight.
My solo routine, a ritual divine,
With every sip taken, I'm feeling just fine.

The Essence in Dark Brew

Deep in the brew, a mystery lies,
Floating like hopes, in caffeine disguise.
A swirl and a sip, what will I unearth?
Is that laughter or madness, a moment of mirth?

The mug in my hand, like a magic wand,
Transforms mornings dull into moments so grand.
With espresso shots firing my thoughts in a race,
Each gulp gets me closer, or is that just space?

Chocolate and vanilla, they flit and they flirt,
Am I just a brewer, or sipping dessert?
The clink of the cup makes a raucous cheer,
As I toast with the beans, a jovial seer.

So pour me some joy in this ceramic dome,
With every warm sip, I feel more at home.
Is it just caffeine, or wisdom in stew?
Either way, I'm smiling with every dark brew.

Ruminations in a Java Jolt

In a swirl of brown, my thoughts start to dash,
Like beans in a grinder, they spin and they clash.
A whiff of the grind, and ideas take flight,
Am I brewing up dreams or just chasing the night?

Each cup is a puzzle, a sip of delight,
Am I finding myself or just finding a fright?
The caffeine kicks in, I start to derive,
Did I order this coffee, or is it contrived?

Between frothed up flavors, I giggle and ponder,
A philosopher's mug, with froth to wander.
If laughter is wisdom, then here I must sit,
Pour another round, for I'm deep in this wit.

So cheers to the jolt, the energy high,
With every warm gulp, I'm ready to fly.
In a world of annoyance, this cup's my delight,
Fueled by pure laughter, I'll savor the bright.

Cupped Moments

In the cradle of warmth, my troubles dissolve,
Can a sip of this magic, my worries resolve?
I cradle my cup like a baby in need,
With every small gulp, I feel less mislead.

The dregs at the bottom, a comedy show,
Murmurs of mysteries only I know.
With each little sip, I laugh and I sigh,
Is that froth I just tasted or my sense of why?

The rhythm of brown, it dances and spins,
Who needs deep thoughts when the coffee just wins?
A chocolatey laugh, like a sitcom's best scene,
Each sip is a story, of laughter unseen.

As moments unfold in this warm, cozy spot,
I raise my mug up, to thank what I've got.
In a swirl of the brew, life's puzzles unwind,
In the humor of coffee, true bliss I find.

Fleeting Time

Tick-tock goes the clock, but my cup stands still,
In a race against time, I savor the thrill.
Every gulp is a giggle, a humorous plight,
As I ponder the meaning, of froth and of bite.

With my spoon like a wand, I stir up some cheer,
The curls in my mocha can tell stories I hear.
A giggle erupts as I slip on the foam,
Each sip feels like freedom, like driftwood, I roam.

The caffeine rushes in, and my worries are clear,
Do I need a life plan, or just one more beer?
In a swirl of confusion, I find lots of fun,
Riding waves of the coffee, I'm light on the run.

So here's to the mugs, holding joys that we find,
In the laughter of brewing, let's leave cares behind.
With every last sip, I'll let my thoughts roam,
In the echoes of coffee, I've finally found home.

Lattes and Lightbulbs

In the café's lively buzz, I sit,
Hoping for wisdom in every sip.
The barista smiles, a latte to brew,
I wonder if he'll spill secrets, too.

Foamed milk swirls in my ceramic cup,
I ponder the universe, without a hiccup.
Each sip like a puzzle, missing a piece,
Is it too much caffeine, or a moment of peace?

The sweet smell dances, like a playful sprite,
With sugar and cream, it feels just right.
What makes a good day? A froth or a grind?
Perhaps laughter and chaos are what I should find.

With each gulp, I chuckle, the quest seems absurd,
I sip on my coffee, a deep-thinking bird.
In the end, it's just brew, but oh, what a ride!
Life's a splash of espresso, with fun as my guide.

Beyond the Brewed Surface

Drinking deep from my porcelain well,
I search for answers, or maybe to dwell.
The steam rising up, like thoughts in my brain,
Am I the only one going insane?

The coffee grounds settle, like dreams in the dark,
I ponder my life, where's the spark?
A splash of almond milk, a twist of fate,
Is my purpose in chai? Oh, isn't it great?

A croissant to crunch, with laughter and cheer,
Every sip adds a story, each laugh sincere.
Could the meaning reside in the muffin nearby?
Or down at the bottom of my coffee supply?

With cream at the edge, I take one more taste,
Is existence just sugar? A caffeinated haste.
I'll toast to the morning, with friends and a roast,
In frothy reflections, I'll raise my glass—let's boast!

Questions Floating in the Froth

A splash of brown, a dollop of cream,
In this bubbling brew, do questions gleam?
Espresso of life or cappuccino glow,
What do I seek? I wish I could know.

With every sip, my mind starts to race,
Can caffeine enlighten? Or just simulate grace?
I swirl in my cup, like the thoughts in my head,
Maybe coffee's a hug, or just beans that I've fed?

Pondering tastes, as the froth begins to dance,
Is this life's riddle, or just happenstance?
Would a sip of dark magic uncork the lid?
Or is it just coffee, life's little bid?

Caffeine whispers softly, "You'll figure it out,"
As I sip from my mug while the world spins about.
Laughter erupts, like bubbles from deep,
In this cup full of froth, I find joy and leap.

The Filtered Journey

A brewing machine whirrs, a lovely sound,
Each drop tells a tale, where dreams can be found.
I ponder my path, over steam and delight,
What's out there for me? Oh, what a sight!

Filtering life like my morning routine,
Deciding what's worth it, what's never been seen.
With cookies and laughter, I peer into space,
Searching for moments in this warm, cozy place.

The pot keeps on pouring, my cup it does fill,
Every sip brings a chuckle, oh what a thrill!
Dare I add sprinkles or a shot of good cheer?
With coffee as compass, adventure draws near!

So here's to the mugs, both big and quite small,
To the people who share and laugh through it all.
In this filtered journey, with joy I confide,
With coffee as my companion, it's a hilarious ride!

www.ingramcontent.com/pod-product-compliance
Lightning Source LLC
Chambersburg PA
CBHW051639160426
43209CB00004B/718